"I've found during a lifetime of encountering helpful tips to encourage kids to enjoy reading, that although such material may be informative, sensible, even well-written, many authors miss the boat in a crucial way. They themselves often lack humor, wit, a well-developed funny bone. Why is this? --when humor is the one thing almost certain to make a book lover out of nearly every child on the planet? Regardless of age, gender, economic circumstances, race, height, weight and whether or not they eat their greens, children become readers when books frighten them, make them groan, weep, feel euphoric or stab them in the gut—but most often and most predictably when a book make them LAUGH, preferably out loud! Fran Hawk not only admires the humorous aspect of children's books, she herself has an engaging sense of humor, and it shows—thus making her audience more likely to remember her tips and to succeed in 'converting' their own children and/or students.

Bravo!

Marilyn R. Mumford, Ph.D.
Professor Emerita of English, Bucknell University

Ten Tips
For
Raising Readers

Fran Hawk, MLS

Pond House Press

Published by Pond House Press, Mt. Pleasant, South Carolina.

Contact the author with questions and comments:
franbooks@yahoo.com

ISBN 978-0-615-29024-9

First Edition
Printed in the United States of America.

Edited by Jane O'Boyle

Designed by Amy Freeman

For Will, Claire, Zadie and Peter
(the current cousins)
and
For cousins to come.

And

For everyone who reads to a child.

"Nothing you do for a child is ever wasted."
– Garrison Keillor

Original publication funded by
The Barbara M. Lindstedt
Charitable Trust
in memory of
Nancy Dinwiddie Hawk
and
John Chrisman Hawk, Jr. MD

"Few children learn to love books by themselves. Someone has to lure them into the wonderful world of the written word: someone has to show them the way."

Orville Prescott - *A Father Reads to His Children: An Anthology of Prose & Poetry*

"Outside of a dog, a man's best friend is a book. Inside of a dog, it's too dark to read."

Groucho Marx

TEN TIPS FOR RAISING READERS
Contents

INTRODUCTION

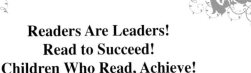

Readers Are Leaders!
Read to Succeed!
Children Who Read, Achieve!

Researchers, celebrities and the education establishment tout reading as the be-all, end-all of accomplishments. They may be right. We may be developing into a nation of haves and have-nots. The "haves" would be the people who have the ability to read analytically and process information. The "have-nots" would be the people who read at a basic level or not at all.

Once you're convinced that reading is critically important, the question becomes how to encourage reading from the first possible moment in a child's life, and then sustain the reading momentum for a lifetime. According to a study by Scholastic in 2006, "Parents play a significant role in shaping their children's reading behaviors…"

Some parents read to their child before birth. Early is best, and birth is early! Sooner is a whole lot better than later. Later is a whole lot better than not at all. Starting to read to your child at any time in her life is beneficial. Forget the guilt trip and begin wherever you are. Whenever I use the word "parents" in this book, I mean for it to include grandparents and all others who love and care about the child.

As with any other skill, it's easy to promote reading when you know how to do it. This book is basic, proceeding step by fundamental step. Each tip builds increasing confidence that you can be a child's first and best reading teacher–and enjoy the process.

Each chapter starts with a "Tip," and a quote to support that initiative. This is followed by a succinct explanation, based on my experiences as a children's librarian, a school librarian, children's book columnist, parent and grandparent. "Be Your Own Librarian" in each chapter outlines exactly what you need to know to find the books and resources that will be most useful to you. My top favorite books are listed at the end of each chapter.

Appendices include more suggestions for books, a quick and easy guide to the Dewey Decimal system, additional resources in print, lively and comprehensive websites about books, and information on selecting magazines.

Happy Reading!

Fran Hawk
franbooks@yahoo.com

TIP #1

Read to babies (no matter how tiny) and toddlers
(no matter how squirmy).

"Part of the whole (reading) process between adult and child is showing the child, 'I have time for you, I respect you, I love you, I care for you–therefore I read to you.'"
Eric Carle, esteemed author of children's books

"At bedtime, taking the time to read a book with a child says a lot. It says, 'This time is ours, just you and me doing something fun together... I love books and reading and I want to share this love with you.'
Picture Book Studio, Journal I, 1985

Our first child screamed with colic for her first five months on earth. I wanted to scream along with her. A loud vacuum cleaner, a shower turned on full blast, a car ride and reading aloud were the only things that succeeded in soothing her tiny tummy. (Drugs and alcohol would probably have worked for both of us, but I was un-willing to trust that slippery slope.)

At the time, I was reading a book about child development that described in detail exactly what parents should be observing month by month. It divided the development into sections for the ahead-of-schedule baby, the regular baby and the slow baby. According to that book, my baby was slower than the slow baby- off the charts so to speak, but off the charts in the wrong direction. To counter my despair, I read to her at every opportunity.

Snuggled close in my arms, she did quiet down, but she didn't evince any sign that she was getting more intelligent. Then, eureka! When I'd been on this IQ-raising mission for about eleven months, I was reading aloud from *Where the Wild Things Are* by Maurice Sendak. When Max waved good-bye to the Wild Things, our daughter raised her chubby little hand and waved good-bye along with him. I felt euphoric and exonerated. Maybe I hadn't failed as a mother after all. Further evidence of this belief was provided years later when she was accepted by the Ivy League college of her choice and went on to finish medical school. So much for slow, colicky babies. Reading conquers all!

Surely your baby will be colic-free and will exhibit every sign of extreme intelligence. You will not be reading to your baby out of desperation. Still, there are compelling, research-based reasons to read to your baby early and often.

Parents may legitimately ask, "Why read to a small child who can't understand the words?" Jim Trelease, the guru of reading aloud, asks in return, "Why talk to a small child who can't understand your words?"

It's important to talk to children from birth, and it's important to read to children from birth. During those early months, the baby won't understand the words, but she'll become conditioned to the sound of your voice and the presence of books.

Trelease cites the work of Dr. T. Berry Brazelton, the renowned pediatrician, who advises parents that their most important job in the early months is to learn how to calm their baby. Babies learn to expect calm and security when they hear a soothing voice. Over a period of months, babies learn to associate the parents' reading voices with a snug secure feeling, undivided attention, and interesting illustrations. The baby is naturally attracted to these experiences. Having worked with countless school-age children who didn't have this experience, I believe that infants and young children make the positive connection with books very early in life. Very early is the very best. A little later is still a lot of good. And anytime is better than never.

On the morning when our oldest child left for college, I was weeping and lamenting that the years had elapsed so quickly they seemed to have telescoped. Wasn't it yesterday that we brought her home from the hospital? Nobody warned me about how fast the time would go. When you think you can't possibly have time to read to your child, remember me on that morning. Childhood is short! There's no provision to back up and try it again.

One of my favorite fathers carries his infant son around his apartment, while providing an enthusiastic running commentary on every object, every sound and every activity. As the baby grunts, the father names the dishwasher, the sink, the round bowl on the counter. Both guys seem completely entertained. That father is having fun introducing his baby to the world. He instinctively knows to talk, talk, talk to his baby. Describe the blue shirt you're putting in that ka-thumping washing machine. Cereal boxes, the mop, falling leaves–name them and claim them for your baby.

Picture books are another way to introduce your baby to the world. Try to find a time to read to your baby when distractions are at a minimum. As you point to items in the book and name them, invite your baby to name them along with you. Praise him for his efforts. Make reading time a time of fun and loving. By including your baby and having him participate, you're telling him that he's an important part of the reading process and that the book is relevant to him. Sometime between 8 months and 18 months, your baby will embrace books enthusiastically. Chances are that he'll start repeating words at approximately his first birthday.

Our youngest child was born when we were living in northern Japan. Our corrugated tin house had one heated room, drifts of snow up to the windows, and icicles from the roof to the ground. That winter, I left the house only when it was on fire or there had been an earthquake. Trips to the library on our military base were an unattainable luxury. With children snuggled on our laps, my husband and I read the Sears catalog aloud, as well as some Japanese picture books that were donated by a friend. The children loved them. What we read was laying the groundwork for imitating the words we said. For the very young, the titles and subjects of the books are the least important aspect of this learning process.

To state the obvious, even very young children have minds of their own. A child may become attached to a book for reasons that defy reason. As you read the same book for the 1000th time, try to take some comfort in the knowledge that generations of parents have "been there and done that."

Protecting books so that they remain in pristine condition is an exercise in futility. My friend who has triplets keeps all the babies' cardboard books in a basket alongside the toys. The boys have complete access to the books. They haul them out of the basket, "read" them page by page, scatter them all over the house, chew the pages and occasionally rip out an especially appealing picture. Yes, children need to learn respect for books. In the early years, though, I favor access over etiquette. The mom keeps the special, more fragile books out of harm's way. One of the triplets' favorite books is the one their mother made from photographs of the people who are important in their lives. The photos are large and safely encased in a sturdy binder. All three boys repeatedly page through this book, naming the people they know and love.

When I was a brand-new librarian and not yet a mom, I believed that young children were attracted exclusively to books with big, full-page illustrations. Along came Richard Scarry to prove me entirely wrong. Although some of his books have large pictures, *Cars and Trucks and Things That Go* and several other of his titles have pages crowded with small pictures that children find endlessly fascinating.

Caldecott Awards and other prize-winning books are considered to be the *crème de la crème* of children's literature. Take time to consider them (you'll find lists online and in every library) but trust your own judgment.

Pat the Bunny by Dorothy Kunhardt was a trail blazer touch-and-feel book when it was first published in 1940. Books for babies have come a long way. "Look, Rattle and Chew!" by Priddy Books is a series of board books with rattles attached that are easy for babies to hold. Priddy Books, with its motto of "big ideas for little people," publishes an excellent collection including cloth books and books that attach to strollers. There are even books that atttach to babies' wrists. Dump trucks and dinosaurs are among the wide range of subjects featured in brightly-colored big board books. Babies and toddlers may not know the "why" of numbers and letters, but they enjoy the books that include them.

The Dorling Kindersley publishing company is another absolutely reliable source for books that will intrigue babies. *Playtime Peekaboo* is a DK board book that combines touch-and-feel with lift-the-flap. Tricycle Press publishes the wonderful series that includes *Busy Horsies* by John Schindel and Casi Lark. If babies like it, it's out there.

Even if you aren't blessed with the gift of a lovely voice (that would be me) sing anyway. *The Wheels on the Bus*, *Picnic Time for Teddy Bears*, and lots of other toddler titles are books as well as songs, and vice versa. There are a wide variety of inexpensive CD music collections for children. Waiting for a red light? Waiting for the grilled cheese to melt? Sing along with *Five Little Monkeys Jumping on the Bed* and the minutes will evaporate.

DVD's and television, regardless of their "educational" value, are not a substitute for books. Scientists at the University of Washington (August, 2007) found that babies ages six to eighteen months knew an average of six to eight fewer words for every hour of baby DVDs and videos they watched per day.

In her Caldecott Medal acceptance speech in 1971, Gail E. Haley, author of *A Story, A Story* said, "Children who are not spoken to by live and responsive adults will not learn to speak properly. Children who are not answered will stop asking questions. They will become incurious. And children who are not told stories and who are not read to will have few reasons for wanting to learn to read."

Brain research and classics aside, your knowledge of your baby is what counts the most in selecting books. Trust your own judgment. All the rest is merely choices, suggestions and advertising hype. One mother told me that her baby was bored by picture books. She decided to read him chapter books. By the time he was two, he'd listened to *The Swiss Family Robinson* and all the titles in *The Little House* series. She reports that he did not like *Robinson Crusoe*. When my grandson was a week old, his mother was reading to him from her dermatology textbooks. At age two, he loves all kinds of books. Whatever works!

Be Your Own Librarian

Although libraries stock many titles for tiny children, you may prefer to purchase the titles most likely to be demolished. Thrift stores, children's consignment shops, library used book sales, and used book stores are terrific places to buy inexpensive books. Also consider used books online and discounted new books sold online at places like The Reading Warehouse (www.thereadingwarehouse.com).

The American Library Association publishes *"Books to Grow On,"* that recommends books for young children from birth to age 3. The titles are listed in 6 month increments with descriptions of a child's awareness of books for each age range. This information may be downloaded from the American Library Association website at www.ala.org.

The ALA, in conjunction with The Children's Book Council, also publishes a pamphlet called "Building a Home Library" which is widely available at local libraries.

As your child's live-in librarian, consult the children's librarian at your local library for excellent free advice on all aspects of children's books and reading.

For ideas on developmentally valuable activities based on some favorite books, try *Story Stretchers for Infants, Toddlers and Two's: Experiences, Activities and Games for Popular Children's Books* by Shirley C. Raines.

Fran's Favorites

All the Priddy books (catalog available at www.priddybooks.com)
All the Richard Scarry books
Busy Horsies and all the books in the Busy series published by Tricycle Press
Appendix One lists additional titles.

TIP #2

Read Mother Goose rhymes to babies and young children
to help them develop literacy skills.

"Mother Goose is your child's first language lesson."
Jim Trelease, author of *The Read-Aloud Handbook*

*"We live in a time when our language is shrinking. The rhymes of
Mother Goose represent our language at its most innocent, playful
and profound. And now they are in danger of disappearing completely. Rhymes that have been repeated and refined for hundreds of
years are no longer being taught to children."*
Rosemary Wells, editor of *My Very First Mother Goose*

Although illustrated copies of Mother Goose sat on her bookshelf, our toddler daughter preferred an academic-looking volume
called *The Oxford Nursery Rhymes Book* by Iona Archibald Opie.
Night after night, I read and sang to her from this book that featured
nothing but small black print on white pages. Thirty years later, we
both remember numerous verses to "A Fox Went Out on a Chilly
Night." Thirty years later, she's bouncing her new baby on her knees
and reciting "Baa, Baa, Black Sheep."
What can explain the staying power of Mother Goose, often
called "the first poetry of childhood?"
To begin, a young child's hearing is attuned to recognize familiar sounds. Children can easily focus on the alliterations, rhythms,
rhymes and repetitions of Mother Goose. There's a musical quality
to these rhymes that reaches deep into the structure of the brain, in
some mysterious place beyond language. This special quality makes
them seem like songs even when they're not being sung. Children
love mastering these rhymes and as they do that, they're learning

numbers, body parts and other vocabulary in an entertaining way. Also, many of these rhymes are about everyday activities in a child's life. "Humpty Dumpty" is about falling. "Rub-a-Dub-Dub" is a delightfully silly rhyme about bath time. Each rhyme is actually a little story. Some of them may help children confront fears of such things as getting in trouble or getting hurt. Other rhymes comfort children.

Although many of these rhymes are very old and have fascinating historical associations, for children they are just a wonderful, frivolous, fun way to learn to enjoy the language. If blackbirds baked in a pie makes you queasy, or a cradle falling from a tree top is an image you'd prefer to avoid, try to remember that Mother Goose is not about the plot. Lyrical language doesn't have to make sense. One of the many charms of Mother Goose is that it often doesn't make sense…or "sense" as we define it.

"Emergent literacy" is one of the buzz terms currently popular in education. Basically, this term reminds us that babies are learning to listen, speak and read from the time they're born.

Some researchers believe babies are learning even before they are born. It may seem that learning to read starts with learning the alphabet, but it begins much sooner. Mother Goose rhymes (and other poetry) help children to become aware of the separate sounds that make up the words. This phonemic awareness prepares them to learn the alphabet and to learn to read.

From birth, Mother Goose rhymes build a child's appreciation for listening and his ability to listen. This is an important part of the process of stimulating language development.

Be Your Own Librarian

Mother Goose is shelved in libraries under the call number 398.8 (right after fairy tales.) Choosing the "best" Mother Goose book is a matter of preference rather than a matter of expertise. My suggestion is to look through several editions and form your own opinion.

Fran's Favorites

My Mother Goose Library edited by Iona Opie
Appendix Two lists additional titles.

TIP #3

Read to pre-schoolers (ages 3-5) every day, at any time of day, for at least 20 minutes.

"Some books are to be tasted, others to be swallowed, and some few to be chewed and digested."

Sir Francis Bacon, 1625

Read with your children because it "...will help them be receptive to all learning, including but not limited to reading. It will help them face life's challenges."

Esme Raji Codell, author of
How to Get Your Child to Love Reading

According to a Scholastic study in 2006, parents play an important role in determining their children's reading behaviors. I think we knew that.

Babies and books grow together. Some toddlers are ready for picture books with bona fide stories, but usually this happens around the time a child turns three. A small child may enjoy *Mr. Gumpy's Outing* because of the colorful illustrations and the animal noises. An older child will understand that the animals misbehaved and will laugh when they all fall in the water. It's the same book and the same child, but the child has a more mature understanding.

Toddlers and pre-schoolers may be worlds apart developmentally, but they appreciate many of the same books. A toddler will love the silly monsters in *Where the Wild Things Are*. An older child will love the monsters, but also understand that Max got tired of the monsters and wanted to come home. Sometimes tiny children love *Hop on Pop* and *Green Eggs and Ham*. Years later, they love these books all over again when they're learning to read.

Assigning an age range to picture books is random at best. When choosing books, consider your child's preferences (fire trucks or ducks) and the length of time he's likely to pay attention. Also remember that one child's most favorite book is another child's least favorite book. No self-respecting child is likely to be impressed with the opinion of a professional book critic. Experiment with lots of titles and lots of different kinds of titles, even books without words.

Although I have more than thirty years of experience with children's books, my favorite two-year-old is utterly unimpressed with my expertise. When he isn't in the mood for the book I've selected, he slides off my lap and stalks over to the bookshelf to make his own choice. He knows what he wants, although his selection criterion remains a mystery to me.

As you read to toddlers and pre-schoolers, they're catching onto the concept of reading as well as the content. They're beginning to understand that books are read from front to back and that they need to be right side up. I've met children who arrived for 4-year-old kindergarten completely mystified by how to open a book, much less what was inside. These children who start behind are almost always the children who stay behind.

Reading was my mother's great escape. She could be sitting right next to me and yet be totally unavailable to me. As a young child, I was frustrated to realize that a book was more interesting and more important than anything I could do or say. I wanted to know what could possibly be in a book to make it that interesting. In other words, watching my mother read made me desperate to read for myself.

I don't recommend my mother's tactics. However, research shows that it's very important for children to see their parents reading. If we want children to believe that reading is important and useful, we have to prove that by showing them that we read. Reading isn't just good for kids. Adults read too, and they enjoy it!

The Educational Testing Service conducted a study that showed students with more than ten children's books in their homes had average scores of 86 points higher than scores of students who had fewer than ten books in their homes. It makes sense that easy, ready access to books is fundamental to reading success. Reading is the critical component of school readiness. When you read to your child, you're preparing your child to be ready to learn. At this age, comprehension is a basic goal. You may ask gentle questions to learn whether your child understood the story.

- "What did you think about the ending?"
- "Tell me the biggest surprise."
- "What was your favorite part?"
- "Did anything happen that made you sad/happy?"

Beyond basic comprehension are the analytical skills, figuring out the meaning behind the actual words and making predictions based on the story.

This may sound ludicrously academic, something only a teacher would consider, but you and your child will enjoy the process. This isn't an interrogation, it's a mission of discovery. It may be a process that you already use naturally. Teachers and curriculum developers refer to teaching children "higher order thinking skills."

After reading *The Saggy, Baggy Elephant* to a small group of children, I asked them questions about the basic plot of the story- the beginning, middle and end. Then I asked: "Did the baby elephant learn any lessons that we could also learn?" That question required knowledge of the story plus the ability to apply that knowledge to their own experience. Following some spirited discussion, it was obvious that the children had absorbed the points in the story and could take them from the jungle and apply them to themselves.

Next I asked: "Do you have any thoughts about why the parrot taunted the baby elephant?" The children were familiar with taunting, even if the source wasn't a parrot. They agreed that the parrot's motivation was probably meanness and jealousy. Jackpot! They are using their higher order thinking skills to draw inferences and conclusions from the text.

My description may make this process sound like a whole lot of work, but children have fun figuring out the angles. They also remember the stories they've explored on deeper levels.

Even with very young children, it's important to ask questions that stretch them to think analytically. These questions teach them to comprehend the stated and unstated messages in their books. Research suggests that children may succeed in learning to read, but start falling behind after fourth grade, which is when the skills of analysis and comprehension become increasingly important. Children who are accustomed to thinking about what they read will have an advantage when the demands on their skills intensify.

The rule of thumb is to discontinue anything that diminishes the joy of reading or causes stress for you or your child. When the book is boring, jettison that book. When the child isn't in the mood to discuss a book, move on.

In a perfect world, each book is merely the first step in learning. *Officer Buckle and Gloria* could lead naturally into exploring police departments or dogs. *Mufaro's Beautiful Daughters* might be the jumping-off place to launch a study of princesses in Africa.

Many publishing companies are providing "extension" activities in the back of their books and on websites. One of the best examples is Sylvan Dell Publishing Company which focuses on nature and math. Their books and their web site (www.sylvandellpublishing.com)provide excellent ideas, activities and opportunities, based on curriculum standards, for children to learn more about the subject of each of their books.

Selecting the right book for the right child at the right time is a challenging assignment. Accept the fact that your child will sometimes hate the book you think is wonderful and love the book you judge to have no redeeming feature whatsoever.

Sometimes I reflexively reject a book. *No, David!* and *Don't Let the Pigeon Drive the Bus* are examples of critically acclaimed books I dislike. Everyone is entitled to his opinion. The important point is to base your opinion on your values, rather than allowing someone else to make decisions for you. *And Tango Makes Three*, by Justin Richardson, is a poignant true story in picture book format that was banned for promoting homosexuality. Just because some parents don't want to read this book to their children doesn't automatically mean that you won't want to read it to your children.

Some of my lifelong favorite books have been removed from library shelves because parents sought to "protect" their children. As a book reviewer for a newspaper, I'm inundated with books I think are awful, books I would never recommend to anyone. Children love *Knuffle Bunny* and *Click, Clack Moo: Cows That Type.* Even though I roll my eyes at the mere mention of these titles, I make myself pay attention and homage to books that attract children's attention.

As your child's personal librarian, you may have your own valid reasons to avoid titles such as *Walter the Farting Dog, Junie B. Jones* and *Captain Underpants.* Children love these books. Should you choose to censor them, just be tolerant of other parents and children who read them with pleasure.

Meet Wild Boars is about a group of ugly animals with unspeakably horrible manners. Some parents avoid this title because they don't want to advocate rudeness. In reality, children love this story and listen with wide eyes, vowing never to copy such boar-ish behavior. A mind is a wonderful thing to leave open.

In summary, Jim Trelease found four factors that were present in the homes of every child who became an early reader:

- Someone read to the child regularly-everything from books to cereal boxes.
- Books, newspapers and other print materials were in the home.
- Writing materials (paper, pencils, markers, crayons) were readily available to the child in the home.
- The child received encouragement to read, write, visit the library, collect his own books, and ask questions.

The National Education Association presents its own "Six Keys to Help a Child Become a Good Reader."

- Starting Early
- Surrounding Your Child With a Reading Rich Environment

• Talking With Your Child
• Teaching Your Child While You Read Aloud
• Helping Your Child Develop Critical Thinking Skills
• Finding a Good Preschool Setting

To all of these suggestions, I add (in capital letters) LIMIT and MONITOR TV WATCHING (as well as video games and internet use). Some TV is good TV. Researchers have found that a five year old child who watches "Sesame Street" is likely to have higher grades, even in high school. Other research indicates that a small amount of TV benefits children, but children who watch too much TV lower their academic achievement. In Northern California, a 2005 study showed that third graders who had TV's in their bedrooms had lower standardized test scores.

What is the optimum number of hours for a child to watch TV? It's your decision, based on the content of the shows, your child's age, your family priorities, and other factors you deem important. From elementary school on, our children were allowed to watch TV for one hour a week. Not one hour per day. One hour per week. This was considered draconian at the time. Now that our children (all physicians and attorneys) have children, they're looking back on this "deprivation" as a positive model.

Be Your Own Librarian

Fictional picture books are usually shelved in their own section where oversized and undersized titles can easily fit. Libraries use different call numbers to identify them. Sometimes they're labeled "J" for "Juvenile," or "E" for "Easy."

For ideas on how to "extend" books, try *Story Stretchers: Activities to Expand Children's Favorite Books* by Shirley C. Raines

Non-fiction picture books (and there are lots of them!) are shelved according to the subject of the book. For example: Dinosaurs in 567; Fire Trucks in 628; Paper Airplanes in 688; Drawing Books in 741. Appendix Eleven lists the numbers assigned to each subject so that the books may be easily located. If your child is fascinated by sharks, you don't need to know the titles of books about sharks. Just head for the 597 section and enjoy browsing.

Fran's Favorites

The Empty Pot by Demi
Joseph Had a Little Overcoat by Simms Taback
The Quiltmaker's Gift by Jeff Brumbeau
Appendix Three lists additional titles
Appendix Eleven lists Dewey Decimal numbers for non-fiction subjects

 # TIP #4

Read fairy tales and folk tales to connect children with
ageless and timeless truths.

*"If you want your children to be intelligent, read them fairy tales. If
you want them to be more intelligent, read them more fairy tales."*
Albert Einstein

*"In a utilitarian age, of all other times, it is a matter of grave impor-
tance that fairy tales should be respected."*
Charles Dickens

After more than two centuries, the pros and cons of fairy and
folk tales are still the subject of heated debate, scholarly and otherwise.

For my first librarian job, I chose a small elementary school
in a rural community where many of the parents were farmers and
migrant workers. I was unprepared for my realization that ingrati-
tude and a sense of entitlement were major characteristics of these
children. Regardless of what the faculty gave the students or did for
them, it wasn't enough. If we had a candy treat, it was the wrong
kind of candy or there wasn't enough of it. Many of the children
seemed trapped in their routine of being chronically dissatisfied.

A friend in a similar situation tackled this frustrating attitude
problem with a direct hit. She read the Han Christian Andersen
fairy tale, *The Little Match Girl*, to her first grade class. They were
stunned, as well they might have been! If there's a sadder story
about a more pitiful and pitiable child, I don't know it.

For the first graders, it turned out to be a powerful magic bul-
let. That story unleashed a cascade of empathy and sympathy never
seen before. Weeks later, the students were still mulling over the

implications. Imagining themselves as "little match girls" was helping them understand the importance of gratitude and kindness. This reaction could probably be expected regardless of the children's social and/or economic status.

Would I read *The Little Match Girl* to a six year old child? No. Unequivocally no. I think it's too sad and too hopeless. Would you? The good news is that it's completely your judgment call.

Fairy and folk tales require painstaking consideration. Obviously, you'd avoid the tales of dismemberment and bestiality, but what about *Little Red Riding Hood*? The wolf in that story could scare the socks off a child who wasn't ready to deal with thoughts of a ravenous, sharp-toothed wolf. Generally speaking, there's wisdom in starting with the most innocuous tales -- *The Ugly Duckling, Cinderella* -- and building from there.

There's a temptation to explain nebulous points in these ancient tales so that our children will hear and understand them as we do. In his book, *The Uses of Enchantment*, Bruno Bettelheim cautions against explaining too much about the stories. His point is that children should be free to derive their own meanings and experience their own visceral responses.

Leaders in the movement for well-rounded education include folk and fairy tales in their reading lists. Proponents believe these stories help to develop children's empathy, ethics and imagination. Far from fostering superstition, violence and illogical thinking, proponents declare that fairy and folk tales open children's minds to imagination, possibilities and mystery. They believe children identify with the characters and find guidance in the stories. The positive outcome gained from reading *The Little Match Girl* to the first graders supports those theories of the proponents. In the words of Albert Einstein, "When I examine myself and my methods of thought, I come to the conclusion that the gift of fantasy has meant more to me than any talent for abstract, positive thinking."

Arguments for and against fairy tales are presented from the perspectives of history, psychology, literature, education and religion. Some critics point out that the tales were written in an outdated, patriarchal society that wanted to reinforce women's relative powerlessness. There's concern that many tales associate beauty with social rewards, whereas being unattractive is punished. Other people argue against fairy tales because young children can't differentiate between fantasy and reality, and thus will become nervous and fearful.

Phooey! Without question, folk and fairy tales are considerably more than shallow entertainment for children. They are integral, intrinsic elements of worldwide cultures and collective psyches. For more extensive and scholarly information about the importance of old stories, including discussions of archetypes and symbolism, the following books are recommended:

Suggested Titles for Adults

Don't Tell the Grown-ups! The Subversive Power of
   Children's Literature by Alison Lurie
Touch Magic by Jane Yolen
Uses of Enchantment by Bruno Bettelheim
The Witch Must Die: How Fairy Tales Help Kids Develop
   a Sense of Self by Sheldon Cashdan

Be Your Own Librarian

Fairy tales and folk tales are shelved in the 398.2 section of the library. Just browsing through that section is productive because you may find wonderful titles you've never seen before and didn't know existed.

This section is particularly helpful when your child is past the simple picture book stage and wants a memorable story with a beginning, a middle and an end–a story good enough to read and re-read.

Because many of the fairy tales are written by either Andersen or Grimm, you'll often be choosing books based on the artist. The following artists are highly recommended, but they are only a short list of all the excellent illustrators.

Suggested Artists

Paul Galdone
Trina Schart Hyman
Susan Jeffers
K.Y. Craft
Jane Ray
Ruth Sanderson
Bernadette Watts
Lisbeth Zwerger

Fran's Favorites

Heckedy Peg by Audrey Wood
The Monkey and the Crocodile by Paul Galdone
Papa Gatto: An Italian Fairy Tale by Ruth Sanderson
Appendix Four lists additional titles.

TIP #5

Read poetry to children of all ages.

"Poetry is the synthesis of hyacinths and biscuits."
Carl Sandburg

"Poetry is especially suited to children. Poems are the cousins of songs and are as necessary in the family of joy."
Esme Raji Codell, *How to Get Your Child to Love Reading*

Sometime around age eight, I was sprawled in my room, reading one of my favorite comic books. Unbeknownst to me, this particular comic was loaded with a subversive element. Right in the middle, between the stories, was the poem "Casey at the Bat." By the time I got to end where the unthinkable happened ("There was no joy in Mudville...") I was hooked. I went running downstairs to share this discovery with my parents, who laughed uproariously and made fun of me for thinking the poem was new.

From this bittersweet childhood event, I learned two things: First, the best poems are ageless. Second, when children make a discovery on their own, they cherish it. Jim Trelease reminds us that children are predisposed to appreciate poetry: "A child cannot help but begin life with a love of poetry if you consider that the first sound he hears is a poem: the rhythmic beat of his mother's heart."

Poetry is so "good" for children, the temptation is to beat them over the head with it. Surprise! That doesn't work.

Subversive tactics, like the poem inserted in my comic book, do work. Pack a poem in a lunch box, fold a poem under a pillow, or stuff a poem in any unexpected place and it will usually be a welcome poem.

Humor (more often than haiku) also works to grab a child's interest. Childhood without the silliness of "Jabberwocky" and Dr. Seuss? Unthinkable. And then along came the poetry of Shel Silverstein to celebrate the silly side of children–and adults. Other funny books of poetry are written by Douglas Florian, Jeff Moss, Jack Pretlusky, and James Proimos.

Some beloved poems have been made into beautiful picture books. *Stopping by Woods on a Snowy Evening* by Robert Frost and illustrated by Susan Jeffers is a perfect example.

Your child will encounter rhymes and learn to identify them in Dr. Seuss, Sandra Boynton and many other books. Those rhymes are important, but they will need (and want) more, more, more.

Be Your Own Librarian

Poetry books are shelved with literature in the non-fiction section of the library as 811. Well hidden, but worth finding.

Fran's Favorites

Father Fox's Pennyrhymes by Clyde Watson
Stopping by Woods on a Snowy Evening by Robert Frost, illustrated by Susan Jeffers
Where the Sidewalk Ends by Shel Silverstein
Appendix Five lists additional titles of poetry books.

TIP #6

Reading books based on math and science will increase children's interest, enthusiasm and appreciation for these subjects.

"Avoid compulsion and let early education be a matter of amusement. Young children learn by games; compulsory education cannot remain in the soul."

Plato

"He who wonders discovers that this in itself is wonder."

M.C. Escher

In first grade, I loved science. Ms. Tarner taught us fascinating facts about the birds that lived in our backyards. Half a century later, I still remember how exciting it was to identify an oriole's nest because it was shaped like a hanging bag.

From second grade on, science was drudgery. Magnets darn near finished me off. Science projects were the guaranteed low point of every year. The USA would have to trust some other student to save it from Sputnik.

Two of our four children chose medicine as their careers, so at least my science phobia wasn't contagious. Now, with a grandchild, I'm positively ebullient about science. Granted, I'm not discoursing on molecular biology, but bugs, bubbles, birds, and beaches are endlessly, scientifically entertaining.

Some of the science books for pre-school and elementary children are shelved with the picture books. Others are relegated to the non-fiction 500 section. Your friendly librarian or book store person will gladly show you the way. These books may be slightly hidden, but your search will reap rewards..

The *"About"* series by Cathryn Sill and published by Peachtree

Press, is a great place to start. For each exquisite full-page color illustration, there is one line of text. At the end of the book, each color plate is printed again with a paragraph of explanation. The series includes amphibians, arachnids, birds, crustaceans, fish, insects, mammals, mollusks, and reptiles. Expect to be impressed!

For children ages 4-8, Sylvan Dell Publishing has a growing catalog full of excellent science books. *If a Dolphin Were a Fish* by Loran Wlodarski is a fun and funny story that teaches children the differences between creatures and subtly conveys the message that each creature is special in its own way.

The Rainforest Grew All Around by Susan K. Mitchell and *The Great Kapok Tree* by Lynne Cherry are perfect introductions to a magical and endangered place.

Old "Satchmo" was right when he sang about the children, "...they'll learn so much more than I'll ever know." This is a good thing.

What does reading have to do with math and science? Everything. With the proliferation of exciting math and science books for young children, it's easier than ever to follow Plato's advice.

Does your first grader grasp the concept of water displacement as a measuring tool? *Weighing the Elephant* is a fun place to start. For hands-on water displacement activities and all kinds of other fun science activities, try *Sandbox Scientist: Real Science Activities for Little Kids.*

What about exponents? *The King's Chessboard* is mesmerizing, especially if you have a chessboard and some rice handy to demonstrate the action.

Children throw around words like "million" and "kazillion," but reading *How Much is a Million?* will make the number real.

Learn about the environment and conservation with picture books like *Farewell to Shady Glade*, and *Turtle Summer: A Journal for my Daughter.* Non-fiction picture books include every subject from hurricanes to house flies.

Be Your Own Librarian

Math picture books may be shelved according to author, but they are often in the non-fiction section shelved with numbers from 510-516. Science picture books are shelved in the 500 section. If you start at around 520 and keep on browsing, you'll find the subjects most popular with children.

Astronomy and Space- 520
The Ocean- 551
Weather (tsunamis, earthquakes, hurricanes, tornadoes)-551
Dinosaurs-567
The Rain Forest- 578
Insects- 595
Sharks- 597
Snakes-597
Birds- 598
Animals-599

Numbers are approximate and may vary from library to library. The people who catalog books have occasional bursts of creativity.

Fran's Favorites

The 500 Hats of Bartholomew Cubbins by Dr. Seuss
The King's Chessboard by David Birch
Turtle Summer: A Journal for My Daughter by Mary Alice Monroe
Appendix Six lists additional book titles for math and science.

TIP #7

Be especially vigilant as your child progresses from picture books into reading chapter books.

"The most dangerous thing in the world is to try to leap a chasm in two jumps."

David Lloyd George

"The more you read, the better you get at it; the better you get at it, the more you like it; and the more you like it, the more you do it."

Jim Trelease

Envision a suspension bridge made of jungle vines, stretching precariously from one side of a bottomless ravine to the other. To progress from picture books to chapter books, children must develop the confidence and the techniques to cross this hazardous bridge. In addition, they need the inspiration and desire to want to make the journey-even though the journey may be rough. According to *Reading Rockets.org*, learning to read is a challenge for almost 40% of kids.

The children on the brink of this important journey are called emergent readers. The books that help them make this transition are called Easy Readers. Sometime between kindergarten and grade two, many children become skilled enough to smoothly decode words and read for comprehension. They may not be ready to read *Harry Potter,* but they are ready to read independently.

Easy Readers are designed to boost the emergent reader's confidence and skills by controlling the vocabulary and grammatical structure of the story. When children read these books that are entertaining and age appropriate, they experience success. They want to read more. And they are safely on their way across the chasm.

Sometimes Easy Readers are criticized for being formulaic and boring. You be the judge. In a genre that includes thousands of titles, the quality varies widely. Because many of the books are in series, they may seem less spontaneous and original. Sameness isn't usually a desirable trait, but when it makes children comfortable, it's a good thing. Children know that Encyclopedia Brown is going to solve the mystery and that Junie B. Jones is going to get into trouble. For our brand new chapter book readers, predictable is okay.

Another approach is described in *You Read to Me and I'll Read to You* by Janet Schulman. This book is a collection of more than 20 favorite stories especially chosen for children in the first few years of school. Some selections are short and easy and others are chapter books. Children and adults may take turns reading any way that suits them.

An alternative to Schulman's method is to simply choose books you think your child can read and enjoy–and read them together. *Freckle Juice* by Judy Blume and *Flat Stanley* by Jeff Brown (both included in Schulman's book) and *The Chocolate Touch* by Patrick Skene Catlin are fun titles for a start.

Be Your Own Librarian

Easy Readers sometimes have their own section, but sometimes they're interspersed with harder chapter books and sometimes with picture books. Just ask. In bookstores, they're often displayed on their own rotating racks.

Fran's Favorites

"Big Max" series by Kin Platt
"Frog and Toad" series by Arnold Lobel
"Mercy Watson" series by Kate DiCamillo
Appendix Seven lists additional titles for Easy Readers

TIP #8

Read aloud to children even after they have learned to
read to themselves.

*"Reading aloud to children is the single most important activity one
can do to raise a reader."*
U.S. Department of Education Commission on Reading

"Do Not Disturb" was the understood, unwritten rule when I
was reading aloud to our children. My husband answered the phone
and kept all would-be intrusions at bay. (In retrospect, we could
have/should have taken turns reading). One school night we were
snuggled up reading when my husband was out of town. The phone
rang on the table right next to us. We ignored it. We were immersed
in *The Incredible Journey* and couldn't leave those brave, stalwart
animals as they crossed the mountains.

The phone kept ringing. Finally, in exasperation I apologized
to the children and answered the call. The neighbor at the other end
of our street was desperate to know if our house was on fire. Her
question seemed exceedingly odd until she explained that several
fire engines, including a huge hook and ladder truck, had roared
past her house with sirens screaming and stopped at our end of the
street. We were so engrossed in the story, we hadn't heard a thing.
Sure enough, when we ran to the windows, we saw that the house
next door was a mass of smoke and flames. Our experience is added
proof that reading can take you out of your own world.

Vacations freed us from rigid bedtime constraints of the average school day. When the children wanted "just one more chapter," one more chapter usually became two or three more. One summer night, the children were tucked into bed and I was reading *The
Bridge to Terabithia*. I was crying so hard, I kept leaving the room

to blow my nose and regain control of my emotions so that I could keep reading. The children were very patient, as they also needed time to pull themselves together.

At around fourth grade, when homework got to be heavy for the older children, I still read aloud to our youngest boy. He would roll his eyes in protest, but we spent some fine evenings in his top bunk reading *The Black Cauldron*. One of my friends is tutoring a fifth grade boy who tackles his homework with dispatch. He knows that the sooner he finishes, the more time he and his tutor will have to read aloud together from *Bang* by Sharon Flake.

Reading aloud before bedtime is the idyllic, accepted norm, but reading aloud has unlimited potential for all ages, times and places. When I was in elementary school, my best friend's mother used to read fairy tales to us as we ate lunch at her house. I loved to go to her house, and I loved her mother. In middle school, I had a new best friend whose mother took us on picnics and read poetry aloud from collections of Emily Dickinson. On a hiking trail in Hawaii, a tour guide was reading aloud to her charges from a travel memoir as they rested on jagged chunks of lava.

When my favorite five year old comes to visit at the end of a long weekday, I read to her while she eats dinner. She's too busy listening to *The Paper Bag Princess* to remember that she meant to stage a protest against the vegetables. Since another book won't start until she's actually in the bathtub, she deposits herself amid the bubbles in record time. The energy we would have used for nagging and whining is shuttled over into listening.

Reading aloud is "Reading Allowed." Any age. Any place. Any time.

Jim Trelease, author of *The Read-Aloud Handbook*, is the undisputed guru and indefatigable champion of reading aloud. After reading his book, you'll be reading aloud at every opportunity.

For some of the children I mentor, listening to a book or a story is a whole new concept. Because they've had little or no experience with someone reading to them, they don't know that books can provide pleasure, interest and entertainment. Because they have little idea about what books provide, they have a very short attention span when listening is required. In contrast, the children who are familiar with books have learned the protocols of listening, which include being quiet and keeping (relatively) still. They've also had practice in remembering what they've heard.

Children who've learned how to listen are ready to learn. This gives them an enormous advantage over the children who are not ready. Teachers commiserate over the fact that when children start school "not ready," it will be difficult (or impossible) for them to catch up to students who started "ready."

Reading aloud helps to build the language skills that are essential for learning. Early reading leads to an early readiness to learn. According to the National Education Association, "Reading aloud…affects children's ability to count and write their own names, which are … important prerequisites for early reading success."

Is there life for reading aloud after children learn to read on their own? Yes, definitely! Teachers and librarians are discovering (and somewhat reluctantly admitting) that high school students will still listen to certain picture books. *Kate Culhane:A Ghost Story* by Michael Hague is a perfect read-aloud for older kids at Halloween. *Sylvester and the Magic Pebble* by William Steig is perfect for teaching the concepts of plot and other literary devices. A good story is a good story is a good story, regardless of the length of the book or the age of the intended audience.

When your child is reading on her own, she may prefer to hear the chapter books that are beyond her current reading skills. Your choice of books will depend on her interests as well as her attention span. When you start a book that is dragging for either you or your child, ditch it! Start something new that captivates you both. There are plenty of books out there and lots of them are just right. The book reviewer I trust most in the world strongly recommended *King Matt the First* by Janusz Korczak. I bought a copy of this out-of-print title and battled my way through it. Even after that investment of time and money, I wouldn't consider inflicting it on a child. Make your own judgments. While trying to keep an open mind, censor according to your own values. Nobody knows your child, your interests and your values better than you.

In a perfect read-aloud world, we would all preview any book before reading it to a child. Although it usually won't be possible to read the whole book, it's fast and easy to check online for formal reviews (www.ala.org) as well as informal opinions by parents and other readers (www.amazon.com). Reviews will often contradict each other, but at least you'll know what's out there. See Appendix Thirteen for more online resources.

Be Your Own Librarian

Because reading aloud is widely acknowledged to be THE most reliable route to raising a reader, there are many books that discuss the various aspects of reading aloud and provide lists of recommended books. *The Read-Aloud Handbook: 6th Edition* by Jim Trelease published in 2006 is the gold standard. Another excellent choice is *Books Kids Will Sit Still For* by Judy Freeman.

Read-aloud guides are usually shelved in libraries with Dewey Decimal numbers of approximately 011 and 372.

Fran's Favorites

The BFG by Roald Dahl
Fablehaven by Brandon Mull
The Goose Girl by Shannon Hale
The Tale of Despeaux: Being the Story of a Mouse, a Princess, Some Soup and a Spool of Thread by Kate DiCamillo
Appendix Eight lists additional titles for reading aloud

TIP #9

Use unorthodox methods and materials to entice reluctant readers.

"A book that is shut is but a block."

Thomas Fuller 1654-1734

"The covers of this book are too far apart."

Unknown

Billy's parents read to him from birth: Check
His home has books, newspapers and magazines galore: Check
He often saw his parents and siblings reading: Check
He went to good schools and had fine teachers: Check
His older siblings are very successful academically: Check
He's been evaluated for learning disabilities: Check
His pediatrician says he's in perfect health. Check
Billy hates to read: Understatement

Reluctant readers are often bright kids who steadfastly resist all attempts to interest them in books. Billy loves his skateboard and plays video games with great skill. All things being relative, books are boring.

Children who dismiss books as irrelevant are a constant challenge to anyone who cares about their futures. My motto is "All's fair in love and war" and this challenge is both love AND war. Bribery, subterfuge, trickery and traps are therefore "fair." Sometimes they even work.

One ferociously hot summer afternoon, I'd taken Keith to a 3-D IMAX movie that bored him silly. At age 6, he was too young to care about much besides the crazy glasses worn by the audience.

What he did care about was a book I'd tossed on the back seat of my car. Even though he's a very reluctant reader and struggles in first grade, I thought he might fall for the distraction of a book on the long drive to the theater.

The book *Where's Otis* by Jennifer Loya had a plastic key attached to the front cover. On each page, the reader inserts that key to find out what's behind the locked door. Keith loved that book. He entertained himself on the journeys to and from the boring movie and was delighted to take the book home. I'm willing to bet that without that key, that book would have stayed on the seat untouched.

Gadget books work especially well for children who need a little junk, an attractive gimmick or maybe moving parts to stimulate their interest. Books come equipped with rattles, wheels, animal sounds, ribbons, stickers, lenticulars (pictures that "move") and countless other alluring gee gaws. Many pop-up books are artistic and fantastic – engineered to intrigue children.

Perhaps it's dangerous to set this sort of gimmick precedent, but somehow I doubt that older kids reading *War and Peace* will expect a set of plastic soldiers to be attached to the volume. Now that Keith is 8, he's moved past gadgets. His current favorite book is Jon Agee's *Terrific*, which makes him laugh out loud. Humor is a gimmick in a category all its own.

Zach, one of my all-time favorite high school students, used to brag that he'd never read a book in his life. I asked him what he thought about performance-enhancing drugs in sports and showed him an article about the subject in a sports magazine. He was absorbed in the article for more than an hour and then drew other students into a discussion of the topic.

Magazines generally provide high-interest, hot topic, short and lavishly illustrated lures for reluctant readers. Magazines are published for every age group, every reading level and practically every interest. See Appendix Fourteen for magazine suggestions for children.

It's a biological fact that boys develop more slowly than girls. From the early grades, boys are more likely to struggle with reading and writing. Boys prefer to be in motion. They tend to develop a competitive learning style that's not helpful in learning to read and write. Reluctant readers, especially boys, may prefer non-fiction to fiction. They would rather read about a rattlesnake than a relationship. *The Guinness Book of World Records* is unbeatable for luring kids into reading. Putting it out on a table is like setting a trap. Other attractive lures are newspapers (especially comics and sports), how-to-do-it books, joke books, and horror/scary books. It's very helpful to provide choices rather than insisting on one specific title. Even kids who hate to read like funny books. Chapter books like the "Captain Underpants" series by Dav Pilkey, the "Wayside School" series by Louis Sachar and "The Series of Unfortunate Events" by Lemony Snicket often keep children laughing and reading. Part of Harry Potter's irresistible appeal is that the books are funny.

Jon Scieszka, the man who wrote *The Stinky Cheese Man and Other Fairly Stupid Fairy Tales* as well as other titles that are popular with boys, has started a web based program called "Guys Read." He believes that the definition of "reading" should be expanded to include magazines, newspapers, websites, and graphic novels–not just books. The website includes several helpful features for finding books for guys that would also be helpful for finding books for any reluctant reader. ReadingRockets.org is another website full of ideas for children who are struggling with reading.

Schools around our country have started programs where children read to dogs. Dogs are patient while children sound out words. Dogs don't constantly interrupt with corrections. Dogs are excellent listeners.

Graphic novels are another friend to the reluctant reader. They look like thick comic books with sturdy covers. Like comic books, boxed illustrations are clarified and expanded by a minimal amount of text. The range of titles is growing and includes everything from super heroes to adaptations of classics. Advocates of this genre believe it's a bridge to traditional literature.

When Billy arrived in middle school, his mother had to be even move creative in finding ways, subtle or blunt, to get him reading.

She was always supportive of her recalcitrant son and stayed calm and upbeat. She was alert for any subject that would interest him enough to read about that subject. From upper elementary grades on up, two of Billy's favorites were *The Darwin Awards* and *Dumb Criminals*, which are found online as well as in book format. He subscribed to "Mad Magazine" which he devoured cover to cover. So what if it's not Dostoyevsky? Not only is he reading, he's becoming convinced that reading can be relevant to him.

Tricks aren't unethical when they cause kids to fall into reading. One of my friends was despairing over her sixth grade daughter's refusal to read. Without saying anything, she put a copy of *Chicken Soup for the Teenage Soul* on her daughter's bedside table. For a few days the daughter ignored the book. Then she began reading random snippets. Eventually she started talking about it with her mom and they began reading the book and discussing it together. Books based on TV shows and movies are often useful in initiating a breakthrough.

Book Camp, or whatever you choose to call it, is another bit of subversion. Put up a tent, homemade or otherwise. Provide a flashlight and explain to your reluctant reader that she may stay in the tent as long as she is reading and as long as there is no talking. The worst that can happen is that she'll stay up reading all night.

My young super-reader friends caution that incentives work better than punishments. Such wise children! They recommend rewards like going to see the movie based on the book only after the child has read the book. For instance, after the child has read *The Lion, the Witch and the Wardrobe*, the reward would be a trip to see the movie *The Chronicles of Narnia: The Lion, the Witch and the Wardrobe*. They also highly recommend time limitations on TV and video games.

If you are really, really desperate, (and even if you aren't) *The Big Book of Boy Stuff* by Bart King may be your best option. It can travel incognito as a Composition notebook or a physics textbook. This is a veritable treasure trove of information about boogers, barfing, belching, and other topics dear to boys. It also has science experiments, games, jokes and advice on emergency situations (e.g.

having a bean stuck in your nose). *The Big Book of Girl Stuff* is equally irresistible.

Parents' intuition is a valuable tool. If you think your child is struggling more than is reasonably expected, talk with your child's pediatrician or pre-school teacher about having your child evaluated. If there is a learning problem, an early diagnosis will be an advantage.

Brain research on reading and learning is expanding by the day. A recent article on the "Edutopia" website states that "new scientific findings spell different, not disability, for struggling readers." As the understanding of brain structure increases, neuroscientists and educators gain more tools to help children learn to read.

"Preventing Reading Difficulties in Young Children," compiled by the National Research Council is available for free online. Excerpts are also available online. *How the Brain Learns to Read* by David A. Sousa is a comprehensive book with free excerpts online. For an avalanche of information, type "Brain Research on Reading" into your favorite search engine.

Be Your Own Librarian

Browse through the magazine section for sports, nature, cars, or any other lively topic.

For children (especially boys) who prefer non-fiction, Appendix Eleven is a mini-guide to favorite subjects and where to find them. The numbers refer to the Dewey Decimal classifications by which the books are grouped and shelved. (If your library uses the Library of Congress classification system, ask for a conversion guide.)

www.readingrockets.org is a website specifically geared to children who have difficulty reading.

www.guysread.com is another website full of reading ideas for boys

TIP #10

Use books in real-life situations to help children make the connection between books and their own lives.

"It is a miracle that curiosity survives formal education."
Albert Einstein

"The illiterate of the 21st century will not be those who cannot read and write, but those who cannot learn, unlearn and relearn."
Alvin Toffler

Cyber, a furry, scary tarantula, was a focal point in my elementary school library. The students watched him with horrified fascination as he ate crickets, shed his skin and just generally lolled around in his cage looking ferocious. Because Cyber piqued their interest, my students read dozens of books about spiders.

The same phenomenon occurred with magnets and books about magnets and paper airplanes and books about paper airplanes. When students saw the crystals inside a busted geode, they wanted to read about rocks. Children carefully carried insects in from the playground when they learned that they could identify them in the reference books.

When I was reading aloud to classes, the children examined a quilt before listening to *The Quiltmaker's Gift.* I passed around pieces of quartz before listening to *Milo and the Magical Stones.*

Connecting the real world to the world of books is a major incentive for children to read. When children are curious and excited, they want to read and hear about the rock or the spider that caught their attention.

Educators sometimes call this process "extension," meaning that the child's learning is extended beyond the pages of the book.

Publishers of children's books can be very helpful to parents and teachers by providing ready-made extension activities. Some of these extensions are online and some are included in the books.

LEARNING SOCIAL SKILLS

In addition to physical objects, children get connected to books through "life lessons," moods and feelings. When your first grader is convinced he's the fifth wheel, read *Officer Buckle and Gloria*. If he wails about being too little, read *Amos and Boris*. *Pierre* is the perfect book to read to a child who is acting bored and indifferent. *The Empty Pot* is an unforgettable story about honesty. *Ruthie and the (Not So) Teeny Tiny Lie* contrasts the pain of lying with the relief of telling the truth. *Those Shoes* and *Four Feet, Two Sandals* give children perspective on the "consumer society." *One Green Apple* helps children feel empathy for a new child at school who is from a different culture. When children read *Something Beautiful*, it empowers them with the knowledge that, they too, can make a difference by volunteering. *Pennies in a Jar* by Dori Chaconas is the story of a boy who overcomes his worst fear in order to give a gift to his father. If bad manners are a problem, try *Meet Wild Boars*. Anger, joy, grief, insecurity, conceit–you name it and there are picture books and chapter books to address the issue in ways that children can "hear." Some people call this "bibliotherapy." I call it a good book.

MAKING THE MOST OF TRIPS AND NEW EXPERIENCES

Prepare for new adventures by reading about them beforehand. Whether it's the arrival of a new baby, learning to use the potty, the first day of school, a visit to the dentist or a family adventure in the Grand Canyon, books get children ready to appreciate and/or understand whatever is about to happen. This kind of thoughtful preparation often diffuses anxiety and creates enthusiasm.

COOKING
(shelved in non-fiction 641)

Our children grew up making bread because I'd declared that sugar was a banned substance. Instead of a birthday cake, the centerpiece of their parties was birthday bread (I thought I was on the leading edge of a sugar-free-children movement. I was actually on the edge of being designated as the neighborhood pariah. But, I digress…).

After I mixed up a huge bowl of dough, the children pounded and shaped it into an alligator, or a turtle or whatever shape they wanted. The only limit was that it had to fit into the oven. The party guests were always impressed, even if they were also nonplussed.

It was my turn to be impressed and nonplussed when I saw "our" turtle featured in the cookbook for children, *Family Fun: Cooking With Kids*. I never imagined that there would be directions for how to proceed and an "unfussy recipe that won't dirty every bowl in the kitchen." Other entries in the "Breads" chapter include "Homemade Pretzels," "Perfect Popovers," and "Quick and Easy Biscuits." As a veteran of chaotic cooking with children, I think directions would be a real sanity saver.

As chinks developed in my sugar-free armor, we made birthday cakes shaped like dolls in ball gowns, popcorn balls, cookies buried in sprinkles, a campfire made with Tootsie Roll "logs" and candy corn "flames"…Mess R us. Fun R us, too.

Incidentally, as the children are cooking, they're learning how to follow step-by-step directions, how to measure, how math applies to everyday life, how to feel comfortable and empowered in the kitchen, and how good things taste when you've made them yourself. Learning, learning, learning – but it won't feel one bit didactic.

GARDENING
(shelved in non-fiction 635)

Gardening has become so widely recognized as a learning tool, it's being used more often in schools. In addition to the obvious science connections, when children see a plant sprout from a dry little seed, their wonder is spontaneous. When getting dirty is sanctioned by parents, children know this is something special.

If our family had depended on our garden for food, we would have been hungry. What we did gain was the knowledge that raccoons like to take bites out of each stalk of corn, turtles like to lay eggs where we want to plant, and all sorts of bugs like tomatoes.

Gardening is a natural way for children to have hands-on experience in "greening" their environment and experimenting with organic methods. Planting a butterfly garden is a great way to jump-start their interest. And the *Good Brown Earth* is a wonderful book to use for background.

CRAFTS
(shelved in non-fiction 745)

"The Festival of Holiday Tables" was the annual fundraiser for a worthy non-profit organization in our town. Every year, about 25 local people were asked to decorate a table (provided by the charity). The decorated tables were arranged in a large room and an admission fee was charged to peruse the results. I thought it was an absolutely great plan, until I was asked to decorate a table. I was bereft of ideas, as well as the commensurate china, crystal and silver. I did have craft books. The table became a neighborhood project. Children created the cloth, the place card holders, the centerpiece, and the china. A good time was had by all, and the table was outstanding (if I do say so myself).

Our family rule was that Christmas gifts had to be homemade. Craft books to the rescue, yet again. Even if money were no object, it's much more fun to spend an hour messing around with paint than looking for a parking place at the mall.

HOLIDAYS AND SPECIAL DAYS
(shelved in the non-fiction 394 section)

Holidays, your own and those of other cultures, are a great opportunity to connect with books. Our family collected Christmas books and kept them in a special box that we brought out every year in December. Although we usually forgot the presents we'd received, we remembered the books as though they were old friends. Because we had friends and neighbors who celebrated Hanukkah and Kwanza, we read books about those holidays to increase our understanding and appreciation of the celebrations going on around us. Books give us an excuse to remember occasions we might otherwise forget. Arbor Day is a perfect time to read *Circles of Hope*. Veteran's Day is a perfect time to read *The White Table*. Independence Day is a perfect time to read *The Star Spangled Banner* by Francis Scott Key and illustrated by Peter Spier.

MEET THE AUTHOR

Local bookstores and libraries offer opportunities for children to meet the authors of their books. This is an important and happy connection for your child to make: behind every single book there's an actual person who wrote the book.

CHILDREN'S MAGAZINES
(see Appendix Fourteen for suggestions)

Children's magazines are terrific resources for connecting children and reading and the real world. Magazine subscriptions make excellent gifts for children from pre-school on up.

Be Your Own Librarian

"A to Zoo: Subject Access to Children's Picture Books" by Carolyn W. Lima and John A. Lima is an outstanding resource for finding exactly the right book on virtually any subject from "aardvarks" to "Zuni Indians." It's shelved in the reference section (children or adult, depending on the library) under R 011.62. This tome of over 1,600 pages is well-organized and easy to use.

The Subject Guide to Children's Books in Print by R.R. Bowker is updated every year and includes almost 500,000 titles listed under almost 10,000 subject headings.

Online, I think the easiest resource to use is the Miami University Children's Picture Book Database (www.lib.myohio.edu). Simply type in a subject and it will provide a list of books and authors, with abstracts.

APPENDIX ONE

Books for Babies and Toddlers   (Children ages 0-3)

Animals Are Sleeping by Suzanne Slade (Ages 2-6)
Fascinating information in a beautifully illustrated format.

Big and Little by John Stadler (Ages1-3)
A mouse, an elephant, tremendous suspense, and fewer than 100 words (one of which is "Yikes!").

Busy Horsies by John Schindel (Ages 1-3)
A rhyming board book that celebrates horses. Also: all the books in this *Busy* series.

Carl's Sleepy Afternoon by Alexandra Day (Ages 2-6)
Carl is a bright, busy, helpful loveable dog. Also: all the Carl books

Cars and Trucks and Things That Go by Richard Scarry (Ages 1-5)
Each page is covered with vehicles that fascinate children and tickle their funny bones. Also: all books by Richard Scarry.

Chicka Chicka Boom Boom by Bill Martin, Jr. (Ages 0-6)
A rollicking, rhyming alphabet book.

Five Little Monkeys Jumping on the Bed by Eileen Christelow (Ages 0-4) Both the book and the song are hilarious.

Funny Faces by Nicola Smee (Ages 1-4)
Masterful use of very few words to tell an exciting story with a happy ending.

Goodnight Moon by Margaret Wise Brown (Ages 0-3)
The mesmerizing rhymes and rhythm of this classic book have put generations of babies (and their parents) to sleep.

Guess How Much I Love You by Sam McBratney (Ages 0-4)
This book provides profound assurance that a parent's love is larger
than a child can imagine.

Hopper Hunts for Spring by Marcus Pfister (Ages 1-4)
Beautiful illustrations and reassuring stories are hallmarks of the
"Hopper" series.

How Many Kisses Do You Want Tonight? by Varsha Bajaj
(Ages 0-4)
Rhythm, rhyme, counting, kisses and animals–all in one delightful
book.

McDuff and the Baby by Rosemary Wells (Ages 2-6)
Delightful McDuff the Westie behaves (and misbehaves) in ways
that make him imminently loveable. Also: all the McDuff Stories.

Moo Baa La La La by Sandra Boynton (Ages 0-4)
Boynton's books are winsome, whimsical and often funny, as en-
tertaining for parents as for the babies. Also: all books by Sandra
Boynton.

Mr. Gumpy's Outing by John Burningham (Ages 0-4)
This is a beautifully illustrated cautionary tale that builds to a logical
and delightful consequence. Also: all books by John Burningham.

Owl Babies by Martin Waddell (Ages 2-4)
Three baby owls worry and wonder about their missing mother and
welcome her home.

Pat the Bunny by Dorothy Kunhardt (Ages 0-3)
Expect to buy more than one of this classic, as children will touch
and feel the first copy into tatters. Also: there are countless touch-
and –feel books available.

Peek-A-Boo by Janet and Allan Ahlberg (Ages 1-3)
There are die-cut holes in this oversized board book that encourage children to participate in the timeless game of peek-a-boo.

Playtime Peekaboo by DK Publishing (Ages 0-2)
Fun with large flaps, hidden pictures and textures. Also: all the books in this series.

Roll Over:A Counting Song by Merle Peek (Ages 0-4)
Laugh and sing with "There were ten in the bed and the little one said..."

The Runaway Bunny by Margaret Wise Brown (Ages 0-4)
This simple book has been reassuring small children since 1942.

Swimmy by Leo Lionni (Ages 2-5)
Gorgeous illustrations and a small amount of text tell the story of brave little Swimmy. Also: All books by Leo Lionni

The Teddy Bears' Picnic by Jimmy Kennedy (Ages 2-5)
"If you go down to the woods today..." Wonderful illustrations to encourage imaginations to soar with the song.

Tickle Tickle by Helen Oxenbury (Ages 0-2)
Very simple for the very youngest. Also: *All Fall Down*, *Clap Hands*, *Say Goodnight*.

The Very Hungry Caterpillar by Eric Carle (Ages 0-5)
The colorful illustrations, the design of the book and the story combine to make this an irresistible choice for children. Also: all books by Eric Carle.

The Wheels on the Bus by Raffi (Ages 0-5)
Children enjoy singing along with this old favorite. Musical notation is included.

Where the Wild Things Are by Maurice Sendak (Ages 0-6)
Children, even babies, love Max and these loveable monsters that "roar their terrible roars" and "gnash their terrible teeth." Also: all books by Maurice Sendak.

APPENDIX TWO

Mother Goose Books

Michael Foreman's Mother Goose by Michael Foreman
Over 200 rhymes illustrated by one of Britain's most celebrated artists.

Mother Goose:A Collection of Classic Nursery Rhymes selected and illustrated by Michael Hague
Rhymes are accompanied by pictures by one of America's finest illustrators.

Mother Goose Remembers by Clare Beaton
The illustrations are sewn by hand using multiple fabrics.

My Mother Goose Library edited by Iona Opie (a compiler of *The Oxford Nursery Rhymes Book*)
This is a two volume set : *My Very First Mother Goose and Here Comes Mother Goose* Illustrated by Rosemary Wells, 1996.

The Random House Book of Mother Goose
illustrated by Arnold Lobel
Lobel is a Caldecott Medal Winner who uses glowing colors to illustrate 306 rhymes.Also: *The Arnold Lobel Book of Mother Goose.*

The Real Mother Goose illustrated by Blanche Fisher Wright
This version was first published in 1916 and has been reprinted more than 50 times.

Sylvia Long's Mother Goose illustrated by Sylvia Long
Whimsical drawings, done in pen and ink with watercolor.

Tomie de Paola's Mother Goose illustrated by Tomie de Paola
Over 200 rhymes with de Paola's distinctive stylized and colorful illustrations.

APPENDIX THREE

Books for Pre-schoolers
(Children ages 3-5 and early elementary)

Adventures of Cow by Lori Korchek (Ages 3-6)
Supremely superbly silly and not intended for instructional use.
Also: *Adventures of Cow, Too.*

Alexander and the Terrible, Horrible, No Good, Very Bad Day by
Judith Viorst (Ages 3-7)
Children of all ages identify with this classic tale of woe.

Alligators All Around by Maurice Sendak. (Ages 3-6)
One of the four tiny books in The Nutshell Library. Others are *Pierre*,
One Was Johnny and *Chicken Soup With Rice*.

The Amazing Bone by William Steig (Ages 4-8)
All books by the amazing Steig are amazing and not to be missed.

Angelina Ballerina by Katherine Holabird (Ages 4-7)
Angelina's adventures are appealing and entertaining.

Animals Should Definitely Not Wear Clothing by Judi Barrett
(Ages 3-7)
Animals in clothing are definitely a laughing matter.

Are You My Mother? by P.D. Eastman (Ages 3-6)
No surprises here, just reassurance.

Blueberries for Sal by Robert McCloskey (Ages 4-6)
A bear cub and a child get their mamas mixed up and then hurriedly
un-mixed. Also: *Make Way for Ducklings*.

Boomer Goes to School by Constance McGeorge (Ages 3-5)
Boomer the dog has a series of gentle adventures that reassure children.

A Boy, A Dog and a Frog and other wordless *Frog* books by Mercer
Mayer (Ages 3-5).
The illustrations will inspire the children's words.

Brudibar by Tony Kushman (Ages 5 and up)
Brave and resourceful children overcome the odds to bring milk to
their mother.

Bunny Cakes by Rosemary Wells (Ages 3-6)
Max and Ruby have very different ideas about the perfect birthday
cake for Grandma.

The Cat in the Hat by Dr. Seuss (Ages 3-6)
Parents and children will recite this book together.
Also: all books by Dr. Seuss.

Changes, Changes (wordless) by Pat Hutchins (Ages 3-5)
Ingenious illustrations tell an exciting story.

Click, Clack Moo: Cows That Type by Doreen Cronin (Ages 4-7)
Children are amused by this tale of what happens when cows became litigious.

Clifford the Big Red Dog by Norman Bridwell (Ages 3-5)
Huge, sweet Clifford has adventures that take him everywhere.

Cloudy With a Chance of Meatballs by Judi Barrett (Ages 3-7)
Children love this story about the random menu that falls from the
sky.

Corduroy by Don Freeman (Ages 3-6)
Lisa and Corduroy, the stuffed bear, are lovingly matched. Also:
other *Corduroy* books.

Curious George by H.L. Rey (Ages 3-6)
This curious little monkey wins hearts and tickles funny bones.
Also: other books in the *"George"* series.

Daddy is a Doodlebug by Bruce Degan (Ages 3-6)
Doodletown is wonderful, whimsical and wholly delightful.s

The Day Jimmy's Boa Ate the Wash by Trinka Hakes Noble
(Ages 3-7).
Hilarity and havoc reign in this tale and the sequels.

Down by the Station by Jennifer Riggs Vetter (Ages 2-5)
Witty and wonderful expansion of the original rhyme.

Drummer Hoff by Barbara Emberly (Ages 3-6)
This rhythmic, rhyming story builds to the satisfying finish of firing
the cannon.

The Empty Pot by Demi (Ages 3-6)
This beautiful and beautifully illustrated story, set in ancient China,
promotes the value of honesty.

The Story of Ferdinand by Munroe Leaf (Ages 4-7)
If you don't mind explaining bullfighting, this is a classic story of
how-to pacifism.

The 500 Hats of Bartholomew Cubbins by Dr. Seuss (Ages 4-7)
This earlier work by Dr. Suess is a story in the truest sense with a
plot that builds and an ending that satisfies. Also: other earlier books
by Dr. Seuss.

George and Martha by James Marshall (Ages 3-6)
These two flakey hippos teach down-to-earth truths about friendship.

The Giving Tree by Shel Silverstein (Ages 5 and up)
A somber parable about a boy growing up as his tree is diminished
by repeated acts of generosity.

Harold and the Purple Crayon by Crockett Johnson (Ages 3-6)
Harold's draws his own adventures that have fascinated children for
over 50 years.

Harvey Potter's Balloon Farm by Jerdine Nolan (Ages 4-7)
What is Harvey Potter's secret for growing balloons of all shapes
and colors?

Harry the Dirty Dog by Gene Zion (Ages 4-7)
Lovable Harry makes life interesting and funny for his family.
Also: other *Harry* books.

Hat by Paul Hoppe (Ages 3-6)
A lively little treatise on imagination and honesty.

Hooway for Wodney Wat by Helen Lester (Ages 3-7)
Rodney's classmates tease him about his speech problem, but cheer
for him when he solves the problem of a bully.

How Are You Peeling? by Joost Elffers (Ages 3-6)
This clever and artistic book teaches children about both vegetables
and emotions.

Hungry Mr. 'Gator by Julie McLaughlin (Ages 3-6)
An alligator is watching and being watched in realistic Lowcountry
wetlands. Also: other books in the *"Mr. Gator"* series.

The Icky Bug Alphabet Book by Jerry Pallotta (Ages 3-6)
Children learn letters and bugs and are entertained in the process.
Also: All books in this series.

If You Give a Mouse a Cookie by Laura Numeroff (Ages 3-5)
Concepts of greed and generosity are presented in this rollicking tale.

Imogene's Antlers by David Small (Ages 4-6)
When a child wakes up with antlers growing from her head, many solutions are offered for her problem.

Ira Sleeps Over by Bernard Waber (Ages 4-7)
This is the ideal book for every child who's ever been both excited and terrified about spending the night away from home.
Also: other books by Bernard Waber

Is Your Mama a Llama? by Deborah Guarino (Ages 2-5)
The right mama is matched with the right baby in delightful rhymes.

Jesse Bear, What Will You Wear? by Nancy White Carlstrom
(Ages 3-6)
Pre-schoolers will identify with decisions, decisions, decisions.

Joseph Had a Little Overcoat by Simms Taback (Ages 3-6)
An ageless Yiddish folk song is presented as an intriguing and colorful story with die cut artwork Also: *There Was an Old Lady Who Swallowed a Fly.*

The Jolly Postman by Janet and Allan Ahlberg (Ages 3-7)
The book combines the fun of getting mail with the pleasure of a good story.

Lilly's Purple Plastic Purse by Kevin Henkes (Ages 4-7)
Every child has been a "Lilly" and/or encountered a "Lilly." Also: all books by Kevin Henkes.

The Little Engine That Could by Wally Piper (Ages 3-7)
"I think I can" is the Little Engine's message that has reverberated

through generations of young listeners.

Madeline by Ludwig Bemelmans (Ages 3-6)
Madeline is a plucky, endearing heroine who's been winning hearts
for decades. Also: all the Madeline series.

Mary Had a Little Lamp by Jack Lechner (Ages 4-6)
A book full of fun that will inspire more creative twists on the nursery rhyme.

May I Bring a Friend? by Beatrice Schenk de Regniers (Ages 3-6)
Rhyming text tells the story of a boy who brings animals on his
visits to royalty.

Meet Wild Boars by Meg Rosoff (Ages 4-7)
These wild boars are wildly, hilariously terrible.

Mercedes and the Chocolate Pilot by Margot Theis Raven
(Ages 5-8)
This book is based on the true story of an American pilot who
dropped chocolate for a German child. Also: all books by Margot
Theis Raven.

The Mitten by Jan Brett (Ages 4-7)
Gorgeous illustrations accompany this tale of forest creatures finding a home in a lost mitten. Also: all books by Jan Brett.

The Nose Tree by Warwick Hutton (Ages 5-8)
Adapted from a Grimm folktale, it has all unexpected twists and
turns.

Officer Buckle and Gloria by Peggy Rathman (Ages 4-7)
A funny story about the green-eyed monster, jealousy, with safety
lessons included. Also: *Good Night Gorilla*, and *10 Minutes Till
Bedtime*.

Olivia by Ian Falconer (Ages 3-5)
All the adventures of this precious, charming pig are perfect for pre-schoolers.

Paper Bag Princess by Robert N. Munsch (Ages 4-6)
This is one self-confident princess who sticks to her principles.

Peter's Chair by Ezra Jack Keats (Ages 3-5)
A classic story about the older sibling and the new baby, with Keats' stunning illustrations. Also: all other books by Ezra Jack Keats.

The Quiltmaker's Gift by Jeff Brumbeau (Ages 4-7)
An irrefutable, lavishly illustrated, beautifully told proof that it is better to give than to receive.

The Rainbow Fish by Marcus Phister (Ages 3-6)
When the Rainbow Fish shares his shiny scales, he wins the hearts and minds of young listeners. Also: all books by Marcus Phister.

The Rainforest Grew All Around by Susan K. Mitchell (Ages 3-7)
Rainforest bugs and butterflies hide in the lush illustrations that depict the circle of life in the rainforest.

Richard Scarry's What Do People Do All Day? by Richard Scarry (Ages 3-6)
Each page offers a myriad of occupations in Busytown, all of which are entertaining and hold the interest of pre-schoolers. Also: all Richard Scarry books.

Rotten Ralph by Jack Gantos (Ages 4-6)
Ralph can certainly raise a ruckus, which keeps children interested in all his adventures.

The Saggy Baggy Elephant by Kathryn Jackson (Ages 4-6)
A wonderful story, especially for any child who has ever felt inadequate.

The Snowman (wordless) by Raymond Briggs (Ages 3-6)
This wordless book with gentle illustrations encourages children to
use their imaginations.

Something Beautiful by Sharon Dennis Wyeth (Ages 5-7)
Even in a dilapidated neighborhood, it's possible to feel empowered
and find something beautiful.

Terrific by Jon Agee (Ages 4-6)
The sarcasm is so heavy-handed that even young children think this
book is "terrific!"

Titch by Pat Hutchins (Ages 4-6)
This is a story especially for children with older siblings. Also: all
books by Pat Hutchins.

The True Story of the Three Little Pigs by Jon Scieszka (Ages 5-7)
Finally, we hear the other side of the story.

Uncle Jed's Barber Shop by Margaree King Mitchell (Ages 5-7)
Uncle Jed is a role model for equanimity in the face of set-backs and
sacrifice.

Virgie Goes to School With Us Boys by Elizabeth Fitzgerald Howard
(Ages 5-7)
Soon after the Civil War, a young girl convinces her parents to let
her walk 7 miles to the Quaker School.

We're Going on a Bear Hunt by Michael Rosen (Ages 3-6)
Children and their dad embark on a pleasantly scary adventure with
a safe and cozy ending.

APPENDIX FOUR

Fairy Tales and Folk Tales

Aesop's Fables selected and illustrated by Michael Hague
(Ages 6-12)
Although not exactly folk tales or fairy tales, these thirteen fables
are an important addition to children's knowledge of literature.

Anansi and the Talking Melon by Eric A. Kimmel (Ages 4-8)
This is one in a series of stories based on the famous African folk
tales about Anansi the Spider

Bringing the Rain to Kapiti Plain: A Nandi Tale by Verna Aardema
(Ages 4-6)
Joyous verse builds momentum as the tale bounds along to its con-
clusion.

Cinderella illustrated by Kinuko Craft (Ages 4-7)
The illustrations in this version are inspired by the lush artwork of
late 17th century France.

The Egyptian Cinderella by Shirley Climo (Ages 5-8)
The absorbing ancient tale is a mix of fact and myth.

The Elves and the Shoemaker retold from The Brothers Grimm and
illustrated by Jim LaMarche (Ages 5-7)
Magical, luminous illustrations bring the story to life.

The Enchanted Wood: An Original Fairy Tale by Ruth Sanderson
(Ages 5-7)
Although a new story, it has all the old elements dear to the fairy tale
genre and perfect illustrations.

The Emperor's New Clothes by Hans Christian Andersen
Translated by Naomi Lewis, illustrated by Angela Barrett
(Ages 4-7)
Both the illustrations and the tale of the king in his birthday suit will
make children laugh.

Goldilocks and the Three Bears by Bernadette Watts (Ages 4-7)
Countless editions of this story are available, but this is an oldie but
goodie.

Hansel and Gretel by Susan Jeffers (Ages 4-7)
This book, as well as every book illustrated by Jeffers, is radiant.

Heckedy Peg by Audrey Wood (Ages 6-9)
Seven children are changed into seven kinds of food in a frightening
tale with a happy ending.

Jack and the Beanstalk by Steven Kellogg (Ages 4-7)
This version features detailed illustrations and a radical re-telling of
the tale.

Little Red Riding Hood illustrated by Trina Schart Hyman
(Ages 4-6)
This is one of the most popular versions of the Grimm fairy tale.

The Loathesome Dragon by David Wiesner (Ages 5-7)
Based on a traditional English tale, this is the beautifully illustrated
story of a princess changed into a dragon

Lon Po Po: A Red Riding Story from China by Ed Young
(Ages 4-8)
Three girls outwit the wicked wolf who is dressed as their beloved
grandmother.

The Monkey and the Crocodile by Paul Galdone (Ages 4-7)
This Jataka tale from India is about a monkey and a crocodile in a suspenseful battle of wits.

Mother Holly by John Warren Stewig (Ages 5-8)
This is a retelling of a Grimm fairy tale about a mean sister, a kind sister, and a crone.

Mufaro's Beautiful Daughters by John Steptoe (Ages 4-8)
Children will recognize elements of Cinderella in this outstanding Kaffir folk tale.

Nursery Classics: A Galdone Treasury by Paul Galdone (Ages 3-7)
Out of the hundreds of books created by Galdone, these are 4 of his most popular picture books.

Pappa Gatto:An Italian Fairy Tale by Ruth Sanderson (Ages 4-8)
Sanderson's art work is museum quality and this story about kindness is ageless and timeless.

Sody Sallyratus by Joanne Compton (Ages 4-8)
This rollicking backwoods folk story is hilariously silly.

Tatterhood and the Hobgoblins: A Norweigan Folktale illustrated by Lauren A Mills (Ages 6-8)
A very unconventional princess saves her conventional sister from the horrible hobgoblins.

Yummy: Eight Favorite Fairy Tales by Lucy Cousins (Ages 3-6)
Familiar stories, simply told with vivid illustrations.

APPENDIX FIVE

Poetry Books
(All age suggestions are very approximate!)

The Bat Poet by Randall Jarrell illustrated by Maurice Sendak (Ages 8 to adult)

The Butterfly Jar by Jeff Moss (Ages 5-10)

Bow Wow Meow Meow: It's Rhyming Cats and Dogs by Douglas Florian (Ages 4-9)

Casey at the Bat:A Ballad of the Republic Sung in the Year 1888 by Ernest L. Thayer. illustrated by Christopher Bing (Ages 6-10)

Every Time I Climb a Tree by David McCord (Ages 5-8)

A Family of Poems edited by Caroline Kennedy (Ages 6-adult)

Father Fox's Pennyrhymes by Clyde Watson (Ages 3-8)

If I Were in Charge, the Rules Would be Different by James Proimos (Ages 6-10)

Poetry for Young People an illustrated series published by Sterling Publishing Company (Ages 8 -12)

Little Dog Poems by Kristine O'Connell George   (Ages 5 -10)

Monster Goose by Judy Sierra   (Ages 5-10)

A Poke in the I: A Collection of Concrete Poems by Paul B. Janeczko   (Ages 5-10)

Something Big Has Been Here by Jack Pretlusky   (Ages 5-11)

Stopping by Woods on a Snowy Evening by Robert Frost illustrated by Susan Jeffers (Ages 6 to adult)

Talking Like the Rain: A Read-to-Me Book of Poems selected by X.J. Kennedy (Ages 4-10)

Where the Sidewalk Ends by Shel Silverstein (Ages 5-12)

APPENDIX SIX

Math and Science Books

About Birds: A Guide for Children by Cathryn Sill (Ages 3-7)
Simple text and beautiful illustrations make this book a stand-out.
Also: All books in this series.

Anno's Mysterious Multiplying Jar by Masaichiro and Mitsumasa
Anno (Ages 6 to adult)
The main math lesson is factorials, but math and imagination combine to make this book appealing to a wide age range.

Bat Loves the Night: Read Listen and Wonder by Nicola Davies and
Sarah Fox-Davies (Ages 4-8)
This story is beautifully illustrated and full of fascinating facts.
Also: All the books in this series.

Beep Beep, Vroom Vroom: MathStart I by Stuart J. Murphy
(Ages 2-4)
A bright and simple introduction to patterns. Also: the MathStart
series.

The Bug Book and Bug Bottle by Hugh Danks, Ph.D.
(Ages 3 and up)
Everything children need to collect and identify bugs.

Bug Fandex Family Field Guide by Sarah Goodman
(Ages 3 and up)
Color photos of bugs spread out like a fan to make identifaction easy
and fun.

The Emperor Lays an Egg by Brenda Z. Guiberson
(Ages 5 and up)
The wonderfully told story of the life cycle of the emperor
penguin.

Farewell to Shady Glade by Bill Peet (Ages 5 -8)
Forest friends are forced to leave their home when construction destroys their habitat.

The 500 Hats of Bartholomew Cubbins by Dr. Seuss (Ages 5-8)
The King orders Bartholomew to take off his hat, and the magic begins.

The Great Kapok Tree: A Tale of the Amazon Rain Forest by Lynn Cherry (Ages 5-10)
Information about the rain forest as well as the importance of preservation.

How Much Is a Million by David Schwartz (Ages 4-8)
Helps children visualize what a million would look like in terms they can understand.

If a Dolphin Were a Fish by Loran Wlodarski (Ages 4-8)
Children will laugh as they learn about the respective classes of ocean animals.

The King's Chessboard by David Birch (Ages 5 and up)
This engaging story clearly and unforgettably illustrates exponents.

Little Panda: The World Welcomes Hua Mei at the San Diego Zoo by Joanne Ryder (Ages 3 and up)
Plentiful photographs and parallel texts provide information and inspiration to a wide range of ages.

The Magic School Bus Lost in the Solar System by Joanna Cole and Bruce Degen (Ages 5-8)
Each book in this series combines an entertaining adventure, basic science information, and how to deal with a student who is irritating. Also: All books in this series.

Octavia Octopus and Her Purple Ink Cloud by Doreen and Donna Rathmell (Ages 4-8)
A fun introduction to colors, camouflage, and perseverance.

One Hundred Hungry Ants by Elinor J. Pinczes (Ages 4-8)
As the ants march, children learn multiplication, division and grouping strategies.

The Reasons for Seasons by Gail Gibbons (Ages 5-8)
Gives detailed, factual information about the seasons on an elementary school level. Also: all other science books by Gail Gibbons.

Sandbox Scientist: Real Science Activities for Little Kids by Michael Ross (Ages 2-6)
Children are learning while they're having fun.

Spaghetti and Meatballs for All: A Mathematical Story by Marilyn Burns (Ages 6-10)
A practical and entertaining "lesson" in spatial relations, with a parent's guide in the back.

The Rainforest Grew All Around by Susan K. Mitchell (Ages 3-7)
Unique rainforest bugs and butterflies hide in the illustrations of this story of the circle of life in the rain forest.

Weighing the Elephant by Ting-xing (Ages 5-9)
A boy uses the basic knowledge of water displacement to outwit the emperor and win back his beloved elephant.

APPENDIX SEVEN

Bridging the Gap
(Children who are learning to read on their own)

All Aboard Reading series Various Authors (Ages 5-9)

Amelia Bedelia series by Peggy Parrish (Ages 5-9)

Arthur Chapter Book series by Marc Brown (Ages 5-9)

Bailey School Kids series by Debbie Dadey

A Bear Called Paddington by Michael Bond (Ages 5-9)

Beginner Books by various authors (Ages 4-8)

Berenstain Bears First Time Books by Stan and Jan Berenstain (Ages 5-8)

Biscuit series by Alyssa Satin Capucilli (Ages)

Boxcar Children series by Gertrude Chandler Warner (Ages 7-9)

Cam Jansen Mysteries by David A. Adler (Ages 7-10)

Captain Underpants series by Dav Pilkey (Ages 7-11)

Childhood of Famous Americans: Ready to Read series by various authors (Ages 6-10)

Danny and the Dinosaur by Syd Hoff (Ages 4-8)

DK Readers various authors (Ages 7-11)

Frog and Toad series by Arnold Lobel (Ages 6-10)

Hello Reader series by various authors (Ages 6-9)

Henry and Mudge series by Cynthia Rylant (Ages 7-10)

Horrible Harry series by Suzy Kline (Ages 6-8)

I Can Read series by various authors (Ages 5-10)

Junie B. Jones series by Barbara Park (Ages 6-8)

Let's Read and Find Out Science series by various authors (Ages 5-9)

Little Bear series by Elsie Minarik (Ages 5-7)

Magic School Bus series by Joanna Cole (Ages 5-9)

Magic Tree House series by Mary Pope Osborne (Ages 7-10)

Marvin Redpost series by Louis Sachar

Mercy Watson series by Kate DiCamillo (Ages 5-7)

The Mouse and the Motorcycle by Beverly Cleary (Ages 7-10)

Nate the Great series by Marjorie Weinman Sharmat (Ages 7-11)

Riverside Kids series by Joanna Hurwitz (Ages 6-8)

Step Into Reading series Various Authors (Ages 4-9)

Time Warp Trio series by Jon Scieszka (Ages 6-9)

APPENDIX EIGHT

Books to Read Aloud

The Bad Beginning: A Series of Unfortunate Events, Book the First by Lemony Snicket (Ages 7-10)
The innocent Baudelaire orphans fall victim to relentless misfortunes that are laugh-out-loud funny and painlessly teach vocabulary in the bargain.

The Best Christmas Pageant Ever by Barbara Park (All ages)
A poignant, funny, sad and happy story that makes us think about the real meaning of Christmas.

The BFG by Roald Dahl (Ages 6-10)
The Big Friendly Giant kidnaps a little girl with whom he has hilarious and spine-tingling adventures.
Also: *James and the Giant Peach*, *Matilda*, *The Witches* and others.

The Black Cauldron by Lloyd Alexander (Ages 7-10)
Part of the Chronicles of Prydain series, full of magic and adventure.

The Bridge to Terabithia by Katherine Patterson (Ages 8-11)
Keep tissues at hand for this book that deals with many issues affecting children, including the death of a young friend.

Charlotte's Web by E.B. White (Ages 5-9)
The most famous spider in children's literary history draws listeners into her web.

Ella Enchanted by Gail Carson Levine (Ages 7-10)
A fairy gives baby Lucinda the gift of obedience, which is also a curse.

Fablehaven by Brandon Mull (Ages 7-14)
A brother and sister share amazing adventures on their grandparents preserve of magic creatures. Also: *The Candy Shop War.*

Gentle Ben by Walt Morey (Ages 8 to adult)
A young boy in Alaska adopts a bear that brings joy, heart break and many lessons about the environment.

The Golden Compass by Philip Pullman (Ages 8 to adult)
Fantastic adventures with a courageous heroine and her daemon familiar. Also: *The Subtle Knife* and *The Amber Spyglass.*

The Goose Girl by Shannon Hale (Ages 7-11)
A princess is demoted to the lowest status in the kingdom where she becomes wiser and happier.
Also: *The Princess Academy* and *Book of a Thousand Days*

Harry Potter and the Sorcerer's Stone by J.K. Rowling
Adventure and fantasy don't get more adventurous and fantastic than this. Be aware of some scary parts.
Also: the entire *Harry Potter* series.

Homer Price by Robert McCloskey (Ages 7-10)
Slow moving but hilarious stories about a boy's life in a small town in the middle of the 20th century. Also: *Centerburg Tales.*

The Incredible Journey by Sheila Burnford (Ages 8 to adult)
An amazing story of animals finding their way home against tremendous odds.

The Invention of Hugo Cabret by Brian Selznick (Ages 8-12)
An exciting tale told in text and pictures, over the course of 500 pages.

Junie B. Jones by Barbara Park (Ages 4-6)
This series about the tribulations of kindergarten and first grade is laugh-out-loud funny.

Lassie Come Home by Eric Knight (Ages 8 to adult)
This ultimate dog story is profoundly rewarding for experienced listeners.

Little House on the Prairie by Laura Ingalls Wilder (Ages 8-11)
Timeless stories that are continued in the series.

The Little Prince by Antoine de Saint-Exupery (Ages 7-adult)
A short, classic story about friendship. Profound in its simplicity.

The Lion, the Witch and the Wardrobe (The Chronicles of Narnia)
by C.S. Lewis (Ages 8-12)
This compelling classic was the inspiration for the movie *The Chronicles of Narnia: The Lion, the Witch and the Wardrobe*.
Also: all the books in the *Narnia* series

The Secret Garden by Frances Hodgson Burnett (Ages 8-12)
This children's classic, first published in 1911 weaves magic, mystery, a mansion and the English moors in a timeless story about two children.

The Tale of Despereaux: Being the Tale of a Mouse, a Princess. Some Soup and a Spool of Thread by Kate DiCamillo (Ages 7-13)
Good triumphs gloriously over evil in this riveting story.
Also: *The Miraculous Journey of Edward Tulane.*

The Thief Lord by Cornelia Funke (Ages 7-12)
Children form a little band of thieves to survive on their own in the mysterious and lovely city of Venice.
Also: *Dragon Rider, Inkheart.*

The Twenty-One Balloons by William Pene du Bois (Ages 7-10)
An entertaining blend of science and imagination, based on the adventures of a man who traveled by balloon in the 1880's.

The Velveteen Rabbit by Margery Williams (Ages 6-10)
A short classic that explores what it means to be "real."

APPENDIX NINE

Resources for Reluctant Readers
(and other readers as well)

The All-New Book of Lists for Kids by Sandra and Harry Choron (Ages 8-12)
Snippets about everything from pizza and roller coasters to voodoo and ghosts.

The Big Book of Boy Stuff by Bart King (Ages 9-12)
Certain to offend some adults and even more certain to intrigue kids.

The Big Book of Girl Stuff by Bart King (Ages 9-12)
Girl secrets, girl emergencies, wise quotes, countless tips and laugh-out-loud funny.

Captain Underpants by Dav Pilkey (Ages 7-10)
A series of chapter books featuring a completely hilarious hero.

The Dangerous Book for Boys by Conn Iggulden (Ages 6 and up)
Includes classic boy pursuits including how to build a tree house and how to fish.

The Daring Book for Girls by Andrea Buchanan (Ages 6 and up)
Advice on everything from note passing skills to science projects.

Goosebumps Series by R.L. Stine
One of the best-selling series for elementary school children.

Guinness Book of World Records (Ages 4-up)
Colorful photographs fascinating extremes: tiniest to tallest and everything in between.

Hands-On Grossology: The Science of Really Gross Experiments by Sylvia Branzei (Ages 9-12)
Everything you wanted to know about ear wax.

The New Way Things Work by David Macauly (Ages 5 and up)
Groups machines by the principles that make them work.

Oh, Yikes! History's Grossest, Wackiest Moments by Joy Masoff (Ages 8-12)
Plagues and poxes, jails and hoaxes- "all the best stuff about the worst stuff."

Oh, Yuck! The Encyclopedia of Everything Nasty by Joy Masoff (Ages 8-12)
Snot, pus, poop and more!

Read It to Believe It series (Ages 8-10)
Relatively easy reading with true life adventure and high drama.

The True Story of the Three Little Pigs by Jon Scieszka (Ages 4-8)
A very funny book that challenges kids to consider whether Mr. Wolf was framed.

The Scholastic Book of Lists by R. Stremme (Ages 8-12)
Trivia, games and puzzles as well as useful information.

The Stinky Cheese Man and Other Fairly Stupid Tales
by Jon Scieszka (Ages 5-7)
Parodies of classic tales such as *"The Really Ugly Duckling."*

Walter the Farting Dog by William Kotzwinkle (Ages 4-8)
The title says it all. And there are sequels.

Wayside School series by Louis Sachar (Ages 7-10)
Chapter book series about a very crazy school.

APPENDIX TEN

Connecting Books to Real Life

And the Good Brown Earth by Kathy Henderson (Ages 4-7)
A gentle book about the cycle of the seasons and the "good brown earth."

Amos and Boris by William Steig (Ages 4-8)
A mouse and a whale learn that size is not important in a real friendship.

Annie Was Warned by Jarrett J. Krosoczka (Ages 3-6)
This is just the right book for a gentle scare at Halloween.

Circles of Hope by Karen Lynn Williams (Ages 4-8)
A wonderful story to read for Arbor Day.

Christmas in the Trenches by John McCutcheon (Ages 5 and up)
A poignant story about the people who dress and perform as soldiers.

Family Fun Boredom Busters: 365 Games, Crafts and Activities for Every Day of the Year. All the Family Fun books and magazines are bursting with interesting, do-able, activities for all ages.

Four Feet, Two Sandals by Karen Lee Williams (Ages 5-8)
Two child refugees work out the best way to share their only pair of sandals.

Lucy Dove by Janice DelNegro (Ages 5 and up)
If you really want to scare young children, this should do it.

The Memory Cupboard: A Thanksgiving Story by Charlotte Herman
(Ages 5-8)
A warm and gentle book for Thanksgiving and for any time a child
has made a mistake.

Milo and the Magical Stones by Marcus Pfister (Ages 4-8)
An intriguing story with a choice of endings: be greedy or take only
what you need.

Officer Buckle and Gloria by Peggy Rathman (Ages 4-7)
An empathetic look at what it's like to feel upstaged and unimport-
ant.

One Green Apple by Eve Bunting (Ages 5-8)
How does it feel to be a new student from a different culture?

One Hen by Katie Smith Milway (Ages 5 and up)
An introduction to microfinance based on a true story.

Pennies in a Jar by Dori Chaconas (Ages 5-8)
A poignant story about a boy who overcomes his fear of horses to
give a gift to his father who is away at war.

Pierre by Maurice Sendak (Ages 4-7)
Any child who doesn't care, needs a dose of this Pierre.

Planting the Trees of Kenya by Claire A. Nivola (Ages 5 and up)
A picture book biography of the first African woman to receive the
Nobel Peace Prize.

The Quiltmaker's Gift by Jeff Brumbeau (Ages 4 and up)
A lavishly illustrated "proof" that it's better to give than to receive.

Ruthie and the (Not So) Teeny Tiny Lie by Laura Rankin (Ages 4-7)
It's never too late to tell the truth.

The Star Spangled Banner by Francis Scott Key, illustrated by Peter Spier (Ages 4-8)
Independence Day is about more than fireworks and barbeques.

Thanks and Giving: All Year Long by Marlo Thomas (All ages)
The title says it all.

The Tenth Good Thing About Barney by Charlotte Zolotow (Ages 5-8)
A very helpful book for children who are grieving the death or a pet or experiencing any death.

Those Shoes by Maribeth Boelts (Ages 5-8)
A compelling story about the disillusionment of "getting" and the joy of giving.

A Tiger Called Thomas by Charlotte Zolotow (Ages 3-6)
A good choice for Halloween and for children who are shy.

Up in Heaven by Emma Chichester Clark (Ages 4-7)
The beloved dog in heaven sends dreams to let his family know he's happy and it's fine to get a new puppy.

The White Table by Margot Theis Raven (Ages 5 and up)
A simple, compelling story that helps children understand and honor our veterans.

Wow! School! by Robert Neubecker (Ages 2-5)
Riotously colorful full-page illustrations enthusiastically promote the joy of school.

APPENDIX ELEVEN

Dewey Decimal Classification System

000-099: UFO's, Big Foot, Computers, Believe-It-Or Not, Free Stuff for Kids

100-199: Ghosts, Dreams, Optical Illusions, ESP

400-499: Sign language

500-599: Math and Science
Space, 523
Volcanoes, Oceans, Hurricanes, 551
Dinosaurs, 567
Killer Bees and Other Insects, 595
Sharks, 597
Wild Dogs and Other Animals , 599

600-699: Technology
Castles and Armor, 623
Fire Trucks, 628
Airplanes and Race Cars, 629
Pets, Pigs, Police Dogs, 636
Kids Cook Books, 641
Paper Airplanes, 688

700-799: Drawing Books, 741
Craft Books, 745
NASCAR and Other Sports, 796

800-899: Poetry-Funny and Serious, 811
Jokes and Riddles, 818

900-999: Wars and Weapons
North American Indians

APPENDIX TWELVE

Books About Books

101Best Graphic Novels by Stephen Weiner

A to Zoo: Subject Access to Children's Picture Books by Carolyn W. Lima and John A Lima

Books Kids Will Sit Still For by Judy Freeman

How to Get Your Child to Love Reading: For Ravenous and Reluctant Readers Alike by Esme Raji Codell

The Read-Aloud Handbook: Sixth Edition by Jim Trelease

Story Stretchers- Activities to Expand Children's Favorite Books by Shirley C. Raines

Subject Guide to Children's Books in Print by R.R. Bowker

APPENDIX THIRTEEN

Internet Sites
* indicates Fran's Favorites

Lists of Recommended Children's Books

www.about.com
Click "Parenting and Family" and then "Children's Books"
This site includes alphabet books, "100 Picture Books Everyone
Should Know" an annotated list from the N.Y. Public Library, and
much more.

www.ala.org
The American Library Association site offers booklists and other
information.

www.cbcbooks.org
Children's Book Council: Includes the American Library Association's list of "Books to Grow On" which is arranged for 0-6 months,
6 – 12 months, 12 -18 months, and 18 months to three years.

www.franhawkbooks.com My own website!

*www.reading.org
 IRA (International Reading Association) : Children's Choice Book
Lists

www.nea.org
(National Education Association) Teacher's Top 100 Books, Kids
Top 100 Books, and other lists including multi-cultural books and
celebrity favorites.

General Internet Sites About Books

*www.bookspot.com
Click "Genre Corner" then "Children's Books." A comprehensive "go-to" site for information and ideas.

www.carolhurst.com
Carol Hurst's Children's Literature Site: Includes "The Reading Skills Pyramid" (worth a look if only because it demonstrates the flow of learning and how skills build on each other) developed by Time4Learning, as well as book reviews and teaching ideas.

*www.streetcat.bankstreet.edu
The Children's Catalog, Bank Street College Library. This site gives bibliographic information and summaries of children's books by author, title and subject.

www.ucalgary.ca
Children's Literature Web Guide: Lists internet resources related to books for children and young adults.

www.lib.muohio.edu
Children's Picture Book Database Type in a subject and the website provides a list of books on that subject with authors and abstracts.

www.school.discoveryeducation.com
Kathy Schrock's Guide for Educators (Discovery Education) This site is helpful for parents because it has an extensive list of online resources.

*www.ipl.org
Kidspace@The Internet Public Library. Links and more links, from magazines to manners.

*www.scholastic.com
Little Scholastic "Introducing babies and toddlers to a lifetime of learning" through articles, blogs, videos and other lively information.

www.thereadingwarehouse.com
The Reading Warehouse is a comprehensive and easy-to-search source for books at a discount, that includes information and identifies books on lexile levels and Accelerated Reader levels.

www.starfall.com
Starfall This site is primarily for first graders and their teachers, but it has fun, educational reading activities for pre-K and kindergarteners.

Internet Sites for Reluctant Readers

www.guysread.com
Book lists and other information that appeals to boys

www.readingrockets.org
ReadingRockets.org: Includes articles about various aspects of reading, strategies to help kids who struggle with reading, books and authors, and podcasts and videos

APPENDIX FOURTEEN

Magazines for Children

Among the most popular magazines for children are:

American Girl (Ages 8-12)
Advice, crafts, laughs and more.

Disney's Princess (Ages 4 and up)
Early learning with favorite Disney characters.

Highlights (Ages 6-9)
"Fun with a purpose" for 60 years
(Highlights web magazine: Highlightskids.com)

National Geographic Kids (Ages 8-14)
Crafts, nature, world cultures, science.

Nickelodeon (Ages 6-14)
Lively entertainment and humor.

Ranger Rick (Ages 6-12)
Information about wildlife and activities about wildlife.

Sports Illustrated for Kids (Ages 8 and up)
Games, players, fiction, advice.

Your Big Backyard (Ages 3-5)
Nature, animals, early learning.

Zoobooks (Ages 6-8)
A new animal every month.

More than 100 magazines for children are available. Libraries and bookstores provide hands-on, page-leafing access that will give you confidence in your choices (The right magazine for the right child at the right time). Websites can also be very helpful in sorting through the bewildering array of possibilities. You may search for magazines alphabetically by title, by the age of the child, by subject and sometimes even by cost.

For each magazine, there's an overview of the contents. All these sites offer discounts on subscription rates.

Magazine Internet Sites

www.magazines.com
(click "children") is my favorite because it provides customer comments and ratings as well as an extensive list of magazine titles.

www.magazineline.com
(click "children") has all the usual bells and whistles with the addition of popularity ratings for each magazine.

www.magsdirect.com
(click "children") also includes popularity.

www.magheaven.com
(click "Browse for Magazines by Category" then type "Children")

www.amazon.com/Childrens-Magazines-Subscriptions/
Attractive format and bestsellers updated hourly.